# Australia

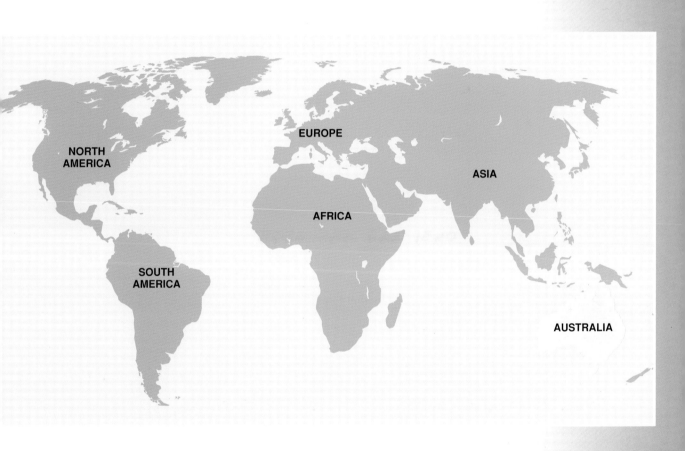

NORTH
AMERICA

EUROPE

ASIA

AFRICA

SOUTH
AMERICA

AUSTRALIA

# Fred Martin

First published in Great Britain by Heinemann Library
Halley Court, Jordan Hill, Oxford OX2 8EJ
a division of Reed Educational and Professional Publishing Ltd

Heinemann is a registered trademark of Reed Educational and Professional Publishing Ltd

OXFORD  FLORENCE  PRAGUE  MADRID  ATHENS
MELBOURNE  AUCKLAND  KUALA LUMPUR  SINGAPORE  TOKYO
IBADAN  NAIROBI  KAMPALA  JOHANNESBURG  GABORONE
PORTSMOUTH NH (USA)  CHICAGO  MEXICO CITY  SAO PAULO

© Reed Educational and Professional Publishing Ltd 1998

Designed by AMR
Illustrations by Art Construction
Printed in Hong Kong / China

919.4

02 01 00 99 98
10 9 8 7 6 5 4 3 2 1

ISBN 0 431 04558 5

0431 045 585 4525

**British Library Cataloguing in Publication Data**

Martin, Fred, 1948-
  Step Into Australia.
  1. Australia – Geography – Juvenile literature
  I.Title II.Australia
  919.4

**Acknowledgements**
The Publishers would like to thank the following for permission to reproduce photographs:
Aspect Pictures, Derek Bayes, p.25, John Earrett, p.23, Alex Langley, p.14; Colorific Photo
Library, Bill Bachman, p.6, Philip Hayson, p.26, Penny Tweedie, p.19, Barbara Wale, p.4,
David Young, p.18; J. Allan Cash, p.11; Panos Pictures, Penny Tweedie, pp.9, 27, 28; Still Pictures,
Mark Edwards, pp.15, 22, Klein/Hubert, pp.7, 8, Gerald and Margi Moss, pp.5, 10; Trip Photo
Library, R. Nichols, p.24, Eric Smith, pp.12, 13, 16, 17, 21, 29.

Cover photographs: Life File and Still Pictures

Our thanks to Betty Root for her comments in the preparation of this book.

Every effort has been made to contact holders of any material reproduced in this book.
Any omissions will be rectified in subsequent printings if notice is given to the Publisher.

# CONTENTS

# INTRODUCTION TO AUSTRALIA

## AUSTRALIA'S HISTORY

Nobody knows when the first people went to Australia. It could have been 50,000 years ago. These people are called **aborigines**.

**Aborigines painted on rocks. These are special places to the aborigines.**

In 1780, an Englishman called Captain James Cook landed on the east coast. He landed in a place he called Botany Bay. After that, Australia was ruled by Britain.

**Australia: towns and population.**

N

Darwin

Townsville

Tropic of Capricorn 23 1/2° S

AUSTRALIA

City Population
○ Over 1,000,000
○ Over 500,000
○ Over 100,000
○ Under 100,000
● Capital
0   500 km

Perth

Adelaide

Brisbane
Gold Coast

Newcastle
Sydney
Wollongong
Canberra

Geelong   Melbourne

TASMANIA   Hobart

120° E                    150° E

Captain Cook landed here in 1788. The city of Sydney grew around a small cove.

## CONVICTS AND SETTLERS

In the early days, **convicts** were sent to Australia from England as a punishment. Many of them never went back. Later, people from Britain and other countries went to Australia to farm and to look for gold.

## A NEW COUNTRY

In 1901, Australia became a new country with its own **government**. Over the past hundred years, many more people have moved to Australia. Now there are 18 million people in Australia.

*Australia's flag is blue with stars. There is a seven-pointed star for the seven parts of Australia. The other stars show the Southern Cross which is a group of stars in the sky over Australia. In the corner of the flag, there is also a small Union Jack which is the British flag.*

# THE LAND

Australia: natural features.

Map labels:
- Torres Strait
- PACIFIC OCEAN
- Timor Sea
- Coral Sea
- AUSTRALIA
- Great Barrier Reef
- Great Sandy Desert
- Hamersley Range
- Tropic of Capricorn 23 1/2° S
- Uluru (Ayer's Rock)
- Great Artesian Basin
- INDIAN OCEAN
- Great Victoria Desert
- Lake Eyre
- R. Darling
- Great Dividing Range
- Tasman Sea
- Great Australian Bight
- R. Murray
- Snowy Mountains
- Australian Alps
- Bass Strait
- TASMANIA
- 120° E
- 150° E

Height in metres
- over 1000
- 500–1000
- 200–500
- 0–200
- desert
- basin
- 0   500 km

## A CONTINENT

Australia is too big to be called an island. It is called a **continent**. It is the smallest of the earth's seven continents.

## PLAINS AND RIVERS

Most of Australia is flat and low, with some hills. There are only a few rivers because there is not much rain.

Much of Australia is lowland. Farmers use the land for cattle ranching.

## UNDERGROUND WATER

There is plenty of water trapped in the rocks deep underground. It got there by trickling down through the rocks above. This water is used by farmers for their animals.

## MOUNTAINS

The Snowy Mountains are along the eastern edge of Australia. The most unusual thing in the landscape is near the middle of Australia. It is called *Uluru,* or Ayer's Rock. It is a rock 348 metres high, with very steep sides. The sun makes it look different colours at different times of the day.

*Lake Eyre is the biggest lake in Australia but it is empty for most of the time. The rivers that flow into it are usually dry because there is so little rain.*

Uluru, or Ayer's Rock, is a giant rock that stands up from the plain in the **outback**. Tourists come to see *Uluru.*

# WEATHER, PLANTS AND ANIMALS

This is a forest with eucalyptus trees. There is not much forest left in Australia.

## WET AND DRY

The middle of Australia is so hot and dry that it is a desert. The wettest places are in the north. There is rain when hot, wet air blows south from the **equator**. In the south-east, it is warm and dry in summer and it rains in the winter.

Kangaroos live in the wild in Australia's **outback**. You can see the kangaroo's pouch and the young kangaroo.

## PLANTS

Only small bushes and some wild flowers grow in the deserts. Grass and some trees grow where it is wetter. There are **rainforests** where it is hot and wet.

## ANIMALS

Kangaroos live in Australia. They are marsupials. This means they have a pouch for their young. A young kangaroo is called a joey. There are also koalas, wild dogs called dingoes, snakes and poisonous spiders in Australia. Rabbits are pests because they eat grass that farmers want for their sheep and cattle.

*Winter in Australia is during June, July and August. This is because Australia is in the southern half of the world.*

# TOWNS AND CITIES

## THE BIG FIVE CITIES

Almost everyone in Australia lives in a city. There are five big cities. Sydney is the biggest with 3.7 million people. The others with over a million people are Melbourne, Brisbane, Perth and Adelaide.

## SYDNEYSIDERS

Sydney is on the shores of a natural **harbour** called Port Jackson. Captain Cook built the first houses there in 1788. Now Sydney is Australia's biggest city and its biggest **port**. People who live there are called 'Sydneysiders'.

Sydney is the biggest city in Australia. The highest buildings are in the city centre.

# OTHER TOWNS AND CITIES

The **capital city** of Australia is Canberra. This is where the **government** meets. Alice Springs is a town in the middle of Australia. Farmers from hundreds of kilometres away go there to shop. There are towns for miners near mines and quarries. One of these towns is Mount Tom Price.

*Coober Pedy is a small town in the south-east of Australia. Just under half the people in Coober Pedy live in homes under the ground. This is because it is cooler under ground than it is above.*

**Melbourne is the second biggest city in Australia. This shopping mall is in the centre of the city. There are no cars in this street, but people can travel by tram.**

# LIVING IN SYDNEY

The Rich family in their garden.

## THE RICH FAMILY

The Rich family live in St Ives which is about 20 km from the centre of Sydney.
Geoffrey and Jane Rich have three children. They are Graeme aged thirteen, Katie aged ten and Jenna aged six.

## THE FAMILY HOME

The family live in a big house with four bedrooms. There is a big garden and a swimming pool. They sit under the **veranda** during the hot summer.

There are good roads and many trees in this area.

# WORK, SCHOOL AND SHOPS

Geoffrey Rich goes to work in Sydney by train every day. He works in the law courts as a barrister. The children all go to local schools. Jenna likes reading best. Jane does most of the shopping in a supermarket in St Ives.

# ENJOYING LIFE

Everyone in the family plays a sport, such as tennis or cricket. The family often go **bushwalking**. A favourite family holiday is to go to the seaside.

Katie plays softball in the park in **St Ives**. Her mother coaches the softball team.

There is a supermarket in **St Ives**.

Jenna goes to a primary school in **St Ives**. Can you see when this photo was taken?

# FARMING IN AUSTRALIA

## OUTBACK STATIONS

The biggest farms in Australia are in the dry areas called the **outback**. Cattle and sheep are reared on these farms. These huge farms are called **stations**.

## GRAZING LAND

Cattle and sheep graze on whatever grass they can find. There are no fields with fences. In very dry years, sheep and cattle can die of thirst if rivers and water holes go dry.

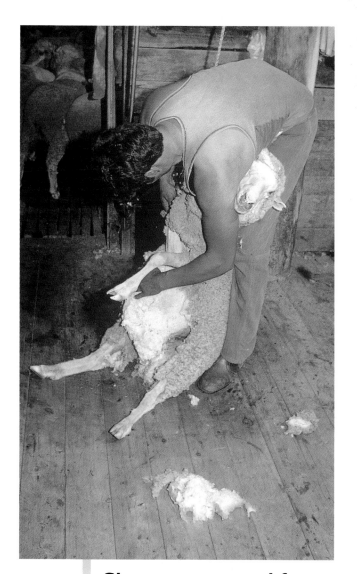

Sheep are reared for their wool. Teams of shearers move from farm to farm to do the shearing.

Wheat is grown on some farms. Farmers use machinery to harvest the wheat.

## FARM WORKERS

**Stockmen** on horseback or on motorbikes round up the cattle and sheep. Another way to find the animals is by helicopter. Teams of **shearers** travel around Australia shearing the wool off the sheep.

## GROWING CROPS

Farmers grow crops such as wheat, cotton, and fruit. Some crops have to be watered because it is so dry. Putting water onto the fields is called **irrigation**.

*There are about 130 million sheep and 22 million cattle in Australia.*

# LIVING IN THE COUNTRY

## THE FAMILY FARM

The Reid family live on a farm that is 40 km from Cowra, the nearest town. Their farm is much bigger than most farms in the UK.

## THE FARMHOUSE

The family live in a farmhouse with a wide **veranda**. They get their water from a tank that collects rain on the roof. They have electricity for cooking, light, heat and for the TV.

**A small part of the Reid family's farm.**

**The family farmhouse. Can you see what the house is made from?**

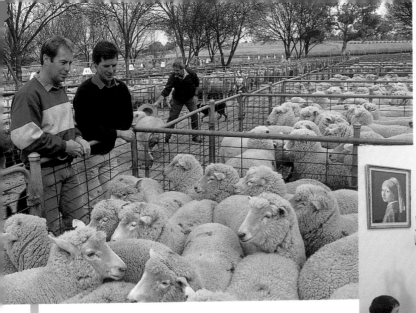

Chris Reid at a sheep market. The sheep are sold for their wool and meat.

Dinner time in the evening when the children come back from school in Cowra.

## INTO COWRA

The youngest children, Anna aged nine and Toby aged seven, go to school in Cowra. Libby, their mother, also works and does most of the shopping in Cowra. Two older children go to a boarding school in Sydney.

Anna in her classroom.

## PLAY TIME

The children have a tree house in their garden. They go swimming in a nearby river. They enjoy living in the country where they have the whole farm to explore.

# SHOPS AND SERVICES

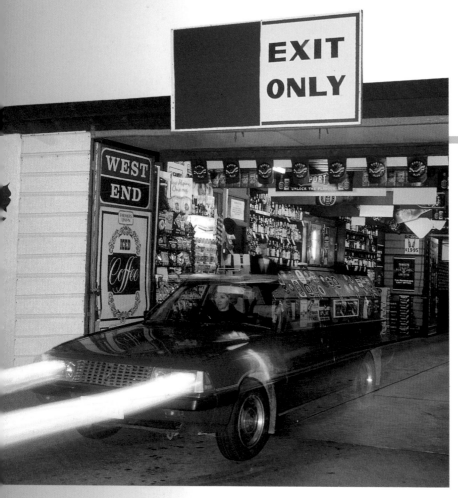

Drivers can buy drinks from this shop without getting out of their car.

## CITY SHOPS

Most Australians live in cities and do their shopping there. There are big department stores and shopping malls with smaller shops. Shops along the roads often have canopies so shoppers can walk in the shade.

## CARS AND SHOPPING

Many people use cars to shop. You can drive into some shops and buy what you want without getting out of your car.

## OUTBACK SHOPS

There are not many towns or shops in the **outback**. Farmers on sheep and cattle **stations** have to drive a long way to these towns. Some fly in their own small aeroplanes.

## OUTBACK SERVICES

If someone is ill in the outback, the Flying Doctor service will visit. Some children live too far away to go to school so they listen to their teacher on a radio.

*A Flying Doctor can get to anyone in the outback in no more than 90 minutes.*

**There is a Flying Doctor service in the Australian outback. This is needed because people live a long way from a doctor.**

# AUSTRALIAN FOOD

## HUNTERS

The **aborigines** used to hunt and collect all the food they needed. This food is called 'bush tucker'. They used spears to kill kangaroos and other animals. They also used boomerangs.

## FOOD FROM EVERYWHERE

People who came from other countries have brought different food to Australia. The English cooked lamb and roast beef. Italians brought pizzas and Greeks brought kebabs. People from Asia brought rice dishes cooked in an open pan called a wok.

**Cooking on a barbecue is a popular way to have a meal.**

This is a Greek restaurant. Many Australian people enjoy eating food from different countries.

## SPECIAL FOODS

Australians can buy kangaroo steaks in restaurants and supermarkets. Freshwater lobsters called *yabbies* are also popular. Fruits, such as pineapples and mangoes, are grown in the north-east.

## THE 'BARBIE'

Because the weather is often warm, Australians like to cook over an open-air barbecue. Beef, lamb, chicken or fish are roasted over red-hot charcoal. A barbecue is also a way to entertain friends.

*A dessert called Peach Melba is named after Dame Nellie Melba. She was an Australian opera singer.*

# MADE IN AUSTRALIA

## MINING

Copper, iron, **bauxite** and other metals are found in the rocks in Australia. Coal is burnt in power stations to make electricity. Precious stones, such as opals and diamonds, are also found in the rocks.

**These diggers are digging bauxite from the rocks. Mining can destroy the forests.**

## SACRED LAND

Some of the metals and precious stones are on sites that are **sacred** to the **aborigines**. Others are on **wilderness** land and in **rainforests** that people want to protect. People often disagree about allowing mining in these areas.

## THE FOOD INDUSTRY

Many types of food are taken to factories. Sugar cane is made into sugar and grapes are crushed to make wine. Some foods, such as peaches, are put in cans.

## FACTORY WORK

Cars, chemicals, electrical goods and many other things are made in Australia. Most factories are in the big cities, including Sydney, Melbourne and Adelaide.

*More diamonds and more bauxite are mined in Australia than in any other country.*

Picking grapes to make wine. The wine is made in a winery.

# GETTING AROUND

## CITY TO CITY

Most Australian cities are hundreds of kilometres apart. Darwin and Perth are over two thousand kilometres away from each other. They are even further from Sydney.

## BY TRAIN OR PLANE

You can travel a long way by train in Australia. The train journey between Sydney and Perth takes almost three days. It only takes 4 hours 35 minutes in an aeroplane.

**A road train is a lorry with trailers. They are used to carry cattle.**

This monorail runs around the city centre of Sydney. The monorail helps keep cars off the city roads.

## OUTBACK DRIVING

The main roads in Australia all have good, hard surfaces. Some roads in the **outback** are only dirt tracks. They can be flooded when there is heavy rain. Drivers in the outback always take spare water and petrol with them. It is a long way between houses and even further between petrol stations.

*The world's longest stretch of straight railway line goes across the Nullarbor Plain. The line is straight for 500 km.*

## ROAD TRAINS

Trucks with trailers are called 'road trains'. They take cattle from cattle **stations** to the city markets.

# SPORTS AND HOLIDAYS

## SPORT FOR ALL

Almost half of all Australians are members of sports clubs. There are clubs for rugby, football, tennis, cricket, swimming and many other sports. Australia's rugby union team is called the 'Wallabies'. A wallaby is a small kangaroo. Australia's cricket team plays test matches against England for a trophy called the 'Ashes'.

The surf boats are used by lifesavers. They are having a race to see which team of lifeguards is the best.

## WARM WEATHER AND SEA

Australia's warm and dry weather makes it easy to play outdoor sports for most of the year. Swimming, surfing and sailing are also popular. Australian yachts compete in 'round the world' and other yacht races.

*The Great Barrier Reef is a wall of living and dead coral. It is just over 2000 km long.*

## HOLIDAYS IN AUSTRALIA

Almost every type of holiday is available in Australia. People can snorkel and scuba dive to see coral and fish on the Great Barrier Reef. Some people prefer to visit the outback or to go **bushwalking**. There are also natural wonders to see, such as the giant rock called *Uluru* or Ayer's Rock. There is even skiing in the Australian Alps.

**Some people like to go bushwalking. They camp overnight in the open.**

# FESTIVALS AND ARTS

## ANCIENT ARTS

Australia's oldest arts and festivals come from the **aborigines**. They made paintings and carvings on rocks in **sacred** places. The aborigines also made their own musical instruments and enjoyed dancing.

This is an aboriginal dance. The dancers sometimes copy the way animals move or show how people go hunting.

## FESTIVALS

New festivals were brought to Australia by people from Europe. Many of these are Christian festivals such as Easter and Christmas.

## THE ARTS

There are art galleries, museums, theatres and the cinema in the cities. The Sydney Opera House is a landmark on Sydney's skyline.

## TV AND CINEMA

Television 'soaps', such as *Neighbours* and *Home and Away*, are made in Australia. There have also been some popular films including *Crocodile Dundee* and the *Mad Max* films. Mel Gibson is one of Australia's well-known film stars.

**This unusual looking building is the Sydney Opera House. The roof looks like the sails on a boat.**

*A boat race in Alice Springs is held when the river is dry. The teams run with their boats along the river bed.*

# AUSTRALIA FACTFILE

## People

People from Australia are called Australians.

## Capital city

The **capital city** of Australia is Canberra.

## Largest cities

Sydney is the largest city with nearly four million people. The second largest city is Melbourne and Perth is the third largest city.

## Head of country

Australia is ruled by a prime minister and a **government**. The British Queen is the Head of State.

## Population

There are over 18 million people living in Australia.

## Money

The money in Australia is the Australian dollar ($A).

## Language

Most people in Australia speak English, with a few others including **Aboriginal** dialects, Greek and Italian.

## Religion

Most people who have religious beliefs in Australia are Christian.

# GLOSSARY

**aborigines** the people who first lived in Australia

**bauxite** type of rock that contains aluminium

**bushwalking** walking and camping in the Australian bush

**capital city** the city where a country has its government

**continent** the largest areas of land on earth, such as Asia and Australia

**convict** someone who has been found guilty of a crime and is sent to prison

**equator** the line around the middle of the Earth

**government** people who run a country

**harbour** an area of sheltered water

**irrigation** to put water on fields

**outback** the area in the middle of Australia away from towns and the coast

**port** a city with docks for ships

**rainforests** the natural forests in hot and wet tropical areas

**sacred** special because of religious beliefs

**shearers** people who cut wool off sheep

**stations** the word used in Australia to describe a very large farm for sheep or cattle

**stockmen** men who look after the animals on a farm or station

**veranda** a shady area outside a house, with a large overhanging roof

**wilderness** remote areas with natural vegetation

# INDEX